CONTENTS

CW00552971

ABOUT PACEY

PACEY is the Professional Association for Childcare and Early Years. Formed in 1977, we are a not-for-profit professional association with the purpose of supporting childcare professionals to deliver high standards of care and learning for children. Our members – childminders, nannies and nursery workers – benefit from access to a wide range of expert support and resources. PACEY membership isn't just about what members receive on paper or online. It's about being part of a vibrant community of dedicated childcare professionals, delivering excellent standards, and together improving outcomes for children.

So, if you're not already a member of PACEY, visit us at www.pacey.org.uk to join.

As a member of PACEY, you make a commitment to your professionalism and the quality of childcare that you provide.

PACEY members sign up to a code of ethics and set of professional standards, helping to demonstrate an ongoing commitment to their career, to meet and exceed the expectations of their regulating authority and to provide the highest standards of care and learning for children.

INTRODUCTION

This guide is to support you in writing a business plan for your new childminding business. It will help you with identifying your Unique Selling Points (USPs), marketing your business and managing finances. We will consider each of these points in detail as we go along.

The guide is separated into three key areas:
Getting started
Financial planning
Support and further reading

At the end of the guide, you will find business plan examples and blank templates. If you choose to use the templates provided, you should personalise the information to correctly reflect your individual business.

GETTING STARTED

WHY WRITE A BUSINESS PLAN?

A business plan is a way for you to set out the key things you would like to achieve with your business and how you can achieve them. You can also use the plan as a way to identify how much you will need to earn to pay for the cost of your outgoings and start to earn an income.

You need to know that your childcare business is sustainable. Give your business the best chance of success by beginning with a strong business plan. A business plan can be used to ensure that you are prepared for times when your business may be quieter (a contingency plan) and will give you the confidence to know that you have really thought about all aspects of being a childminder. By recording the information in a formal document you are showing that you are serious about your business.

Over time, your business plan may change and develop as you and your business change, and you will need to regularly review and update your plan. It is important to recognise that you will be entering a competitive market and you need to be fully prepared with as much information as possible to help you succeed.

Don't be afraid!

Writing a business plan for the first time can be daunting, but remember – we all financially plan in our daily lives; we think about how much household income we receive and how much we will need to cover our expenses such as bills and food shopping. We then plan to save any excess money for a "rainy day" or a treat such as a holiday. If we find that we do not have enough money coming in, we think about how we can cut back on our spending.

HOW TO WRITE A BUSINESS PLAN

Start with a short description, or overview, of your business. Remember to include the basics: your name, your business name, address and contact details. Describe what your business will offer. For example, the ages of the children you intend to care for and hours you are going to be available. Include in this section any information about assistants or other childminders you may wish to work with.

You should also include a few sentences about your goals for your business, both for the short term and for the future. For example, you could set out what you would like your business to achieve in six months' time, a year's time and three years' time. When considering your aims and objectives, make sure you set yourself SMART targets (Specific, Measurable, Achievable, Realistic, Time).

Specific	What do you want to achieve? Make it specific and focused
Measurable	How will you monitor progress and know if you have been successful?
Achievable	You should not set yourself up to fail; targets need to be challenging, but also possible with commitment
Realistic	Have you got the necessary skills, knowledge, experience, equipment and funding to achieve your target?
Time	Give a date by which you should have met your targets. This will help you to keep focused

An example of a SMART target for a new childminding business could be to have 75 per cent occupancy within a year and to have achieved a "good" in your first post-registration Ofsted inspection (England only). Create a SMART target and timescale that you feel is achievable. This will be influenced by your market research and potential customers (see pages 12 to 17).

You could also add information about why you decided to become a childminder and the skills that you have. You may find it beneficial to record this information as a reminder for your future development.

Pre-registration training

Before registering as a childminder, there are certain pre-registration courses to complete. Visit **www.pacey.org.uk/businessbasics** to find out more about pre-registration training and registering as a childminder.

Take a look at the table opposite. This shows an example of how you may decide to show relevant information on education, qualifications and experience in your business plan. If you are going to be working with an assistant or other childminder, include information about their experience and qualifications, too.

The list opposite is not exhaustive, but is given as a starting point. Think about your business and add anything that enables the reader to have a clear picture of you and your business.

QUALIFICATIONS, TRAINING AND EXPERIENCE	DATE ACHIEVED	RENEWAL DATE
Childcare qualification (level 2,3,4 etc.)		
CYPOP5		
Other accredited module		
Paediatric First Aid		
Child Protection		
Food Hygiene		
Health and Safety		
SENCO training		
Equalities training		
Child development training		
Any additional training		
Relevant experience		

DBS NUMBER	DATE RECEIVED

Ofsted registration number and grade of last inspection (England) or CSSIW registration number and date of last inspection (Wales)	REGISTRATION NUMBER	GRADE (ENGLAND ONLY)

SWOT ANALYSIS

It is useful to carry out a Strengths, Weaknesses, Opportunities and Threats (SWOT) analysis when planning for your future business. This will enable you to plan for your future business development and identify possible threats to your business.

Strengths — What do you do well? What are your unique selling points (USPs) that set you apart from other childcare providers?

Weaknesses — What do you need to improve? What areas are you less confident with?

Opportunities — What can you use to develop your business and your knowledge?

Threats — What might affect your future success? What changes might happen to your business?

Strengths and weaknesses are about you as a childcare provider, whilst opportunities and threats allow you to consider external influences. Once you have completed a SWOT analysis, use the information to help you decide what to do next: you could communicate your strengths to potential customers through your marketing materials; think about how to improve in areas you are less confident with; and research how to access and make the most of any available opportunities.

Consider whether there is anything you can do to protect your business against external threats. For example, is there something you can offer that other childcare providers may not? See page 12 to find out about USPs. Consider what course of action you may need to take if any threats arise.

The examples on page 44 demonstrate the range of information you can include in your SWOT analysis. Remember that yours will be unique to you and your childcare practice

MARKET RESEARCH

It is important to have a clear marketing strategy for your business and a good understanding of the market that you will be entering. Your business is childcare and your market prospective parents. You need to be confident that there are sufficient children in your area that may require your service to ensure that your business is sustainable.

It is also important to identify your possible competitors. For childminders, these will be other childcare providers such as day nurseries, other childminders, nannies, and before-and-after school clubs. Consider how your service is going to be the one that families choose and how you will market your business.

Unique Selling Points (USPs)

Next, think about your **USPs**. These are the things that will make your service individual to you and make you stand out from the crowd. Your USPs might be your experience, skills and knowledge, the environment you are going to offer your service from, or the hours in which your service will be available, or a combination of these. The page opposite shows some examples of USPs. Remember that each business will have its own USPs, so think about your childcare practice and what makes you unique and appealing to parents.

Example 1 – Experienced early years professional with in-depth knowledge of how young children learn and develop

Example 2 – Home-based childcare, with playroom and extensive outside area, including sand play, climbing equipment and wheeled toys

Example 3 – Available to take to and collect from local school in rural area

Example 4 – Extended hours to meet the needs of working families, overnight care available

Example 5 – Fluent Welsh speaker, extending Welsh language opportunities through Welsh medium parent and toddler groups

" We provide care for children with disabilities, we find it so rewarding for us and all the children in our care "

Karen Gallimore, Flintshire

Customers

The next step is to find who and where your potential customers are. For your business to be a success, you need to be sure that there is a demand in your area for your service.

It is important to identify what your customers want. If families would like a childminder who collects from one local school and you do not offer this service, you may struggle to fill places as you will not meet the needs of your market. By understanding the needs of your potential customers, you can tailor your service to meet these needs. This will help you to establish a successful and sustainable business. You could start by asking potential customers about their requirements.

This could include:
- Questionnaires for parents
- Informal interviews
- Discussions
- Online forums

All of these methods could be used to gather relevant and useful information and time should be given to gather this information thoroughly and to analyse the results.

Competitors

Find out about other childcare providers in your area and think about your services in relation to these providers. Collect information about their location, prices, services offered and the quality of the provision.

This can be done by looking at information provided on their websites and talking with people who have used their services. You could also look in local business directories and gain information from your local Family Information Service (FIS).

You can look at the type of care offered by competitors by reading Ofsted inspection reports in England (available at **www.ofsted.gov.uk**) or CSSIW inspection reports in Wales (available at **www.cssiw.org.uk**). Please note the exception to this is that in Wales registered childminder reports are not currently available online; copies have to be requested.

In Wales, you can research your local childcare sufficiency assessment to understand the need for childcare in your area.

MARKETING YOUR BUSINESS

Now that you have established your USPs and potential customers, it's time to let people know about your business, and there are many ways in which you can do this. Make a marketing plan, detailing how you are going to reach your potential customers. This may include advertising and promoting your business.

Use the information gathered in your market research to ensure that your marketing is appropriate to your audience. Your USPs and information about customer requirements can be used to tailor your marketing, enabling you to appeal to and contact potential customers. Use your SWOT analysis to identify your strengths and opportunities.

Remember to budget for marketing and, crucially, allow time for it.

Your audience

You will already have decided upon your audience in your market research stage. Now think about how to get a message across to those parents. Are you aiming for children of similar or different ages? There may be several ways to reach your varied audiences, and it sometimes helps to create profiles of the type of parent you are trying to market to. As an example:

Eva and John are parents to twin girls, aged 2. They need childcare for three afternoons a week.

Sunny and Mizan are both working locally. They are looking for full-time childcare for Charlie, aged 3, who has been diagnosed with autism.

Janelle is a single parent with a high-powered job. She needs after-school care and occasional overnight help for Aiden, aged 5.

Marketing channels

How would you target these individuals? Would they need different methods and channels of communication? Would they be looking for different messages about the areas of expertise that you offer?

For example, Eva and John may look at your advert on the wall at the local soft play centre where they take their daughters; Sunny and Mizan might pick up the leaflet you drop through their door; and Janelle may be more likely to search for childcare through an online vacancy matching service.

These parents are all in your local area, but have different requirements and you could use a number of different ways to reach them.

When you have identified the types of parents in your overall market, you can identify the appropriate marketing channels to reach them, from display advertising to word of mouth. Turn the page to see some examples of different marketing channels.

ADVERTISING IN THE COMMUNITY

This means signs or posters or cards – these could be put up in:
- Cafés
- Play centres
- Children's centres
- Schools
- Supermarkets and local shops
- Doctors' surgeries
- Specialist children's clinics

Be careful to always ask permission – some places will charge – and do not fly-post.

DISPLAY ADVERTISING – PRINT OR DIGITAL

This means in directories or other places designed to sell services, for example:
- Local directories (online or print)
- Advertising online in local forums
- Advertising online with vacancy matching services

Local directories may list your business for free, with larger advertising spaces available at a cost. The more your company name and/or website are referenced online, the more they will appear in search engine results, helping people to find you.

If you are a childminder member of PACEY, you have access to a free vacancy matching service where you can advertise your business to parents. Visit **www.pacey.org.uk/vacancies** to find out more. You will need your membership details to hand.

Don't forget to contact your local FIS, too, to see how they can help.

RUN OF PAPER ADVERTISING

This means in places where people will see it as they read/look at something else, such as advertising in:
- Local papers
- Local magazines
- School or club newsletters (such as Brownies, Cubs, Scouts, Guides, gyms or play clubs)

DIRECT MAIL

This is when you go to potential customers in a direct way – either in print or digitally. For example:
- Door drops of leaflets in your catchment area (through letterboxes)
- A paragraph in a school email
- Brochure inserts in a local fair or theatre goody bag
- Letters by post or email to a local newsletter audience (with permission)

Be prepared, though – an average direct mail may only produce four leads (interested parents) out of every 100 letters that you send.*

You could ask your local business advice centre or friends if you need advice on mail-merging documents.

EVENTS

You can often promote your services, at a cost, at things like local fairs or specialist parent events. If you do this, it is a good idea to have some leaflets and business cards to give parents and a poster or stand behind you. Sweets or cakes will often encourage people to come to your stand!

* Source: The Direct Marketing Association (DMA) 2012 Response Rate Report

SOCIAL MEDIA

This is using today's online networks to promote your business, for example:

- Creating and using your own Facebook page and LinkedIn profiles
- Blogging or posting on parent forums
- Promoting your business through feeds such as Twitter or similar

Don't forget to be careful about permissions and safeguarding issues – don't post photographs of children online or in advertising without written permission from parents, and be careful with what you post. For more information about data protection, visit the Information Commissioner's Office at **www.ico.org.uk**

BUSINESS CARDS AND WORD OF MOUTH

Always ensure you have business cards on-hand as they provide an easy way to contact you. Why not give them to your friends and family to hand out, too? Word of mouth is often the best way to get good recommendations and you never know when you, or people you know, will chat to someone who needs childcare. Business cards can be produced very cheaply using online printers. You could also encourage customers to introduce other families to your business by rewarding them with something simple, like a voucher.

Remember, advertising and brochures must be true, fair and not misleading. To find out more about advertising regulations and codes of practice, visit www.gov.uk/marketing-advertising-law

Marketing tactics

Tactics means thinking about which channels to use and when. You may wish to do more marketing activity before the school holidays end if you are focusing on after-school care. Or, if you know a nursery is closing for refurbishment, this could be a good time to do a door drop in the area to perhaps offer interim support.

Your message is also an important part of marketing tactics. Telling a parent with a 3-year-old that you have experience of caring for babies isn't a useful message, but telling them you have completed child development training is a really useful one that might win you business.

Don't forget to also think about ways to encourage your audience to respond to you as soon as possible. Special offers, such as money off the first month, can be very effective.

" I went along to local toddler groups and chatted to mothers at school gates. I always drop into conversations that I am a childminder. Word of mouth is invaluable! **"**

Holly Love, Monmouthshire

Measurement

In order to decide what marketing is working for you and what isn't, try to keep track of where your enquiries and, importantly, actual placements come from. That way, you will be able to see the most effective marketing channel in *your area, for your audience*, and *when* those marketing channels work best. This will help you to spend any money on the type of marketing that has been most successful for you, and should mean quicker results in the future.

Key messages

Here are five things to remember when marketing your business:

- Make sure you get across the key message to each audience – whether that is that you offer specialised care, wrap-around care, speaking more than one language, or simply excellent childcare!
- Include a 'call to action' (what the parent should do next to get in touch)
- Be easily contactable, whichever way works best for you and, importantly, for your audience
- Don't include your full address and EY number (England) when designing posters and advertisements to protect you, your family and the childminded children
- Check and double-check your contact details

FINANCIAL
PLANNING

EXPENDITURE

The next section of your business plan needs to be a clear understanding of your finances. A successful business does not just need a high-quality service but also good financial planning. It's essential to understand your outgoings (expenditure) and the money you have coming in (income) to make a forecast of how your business will develop.

Start-up costs

When writing your finance plan, consider your start-up costs. These will be different for every setting, but the table below is a starting point to provide you with some ideas of what to consider. Some start-up costs and regular costs (e.g. weekly costs) are allowable expenses. You can find out more on page 30.

START-UP COSTS	EXAMPLES	EXPENDITURE
Training	CYPOP5, Paediatric First Aid, Food Hygiene, Safeguarding	£
Ofsted / CSSIW	Registration / DBS check	£
Marketing	Advertising, flyers, website	£
Equipment and resources	Toys, books, outside equipment, car seats, pushchairs, highchair, cutlery, plates, cups, bowls, bottles, nappy changing equipment, potty, IT equipment	£
Alterations to premises*	Access changes, safety requirements	£
Recruitment	Assistant, other childminder	£
Professional fees	Accountant, registration with Information Commissioner's Office (ICO)	£
Support	PACEY membership, toy library membership	£
Insurance	Car insurance, home insurance and Public Liability Insurance (PLI)	£

*If all relevant permissions have been granted by your local authority.

Weekly costs

The next step is to work out your ongoing expenditure. Work out your weekly expenditure and a forecast for the year ahead. Annual costs could be calculated and then divided by 52 to show the weekly proportion of that cost. Expenses may be small or large amounts and will need to include any personal expenses and business expenses. The table below shows examples of costs you might need to consider.

EXAMPLES	ANNUAL EXPENDITURE	WEEKLY PROPORTION
Rent / mortgage	£	£
Council tax	£	£
Utility bills	£	£
Telephone, mobile, internet	£	£
Insurances	£	£
Food	£	£
Car costs, fuel	£	£
Personal expenditure e.g. clothes, gifts, holidays	£	£
Subscriptions	£	£
Training	£	£
PACEY membership and insurance	£	£
Ofsted (If registering with CSSIW in Wales there is currently no charge)	£	£
Professional fees	£	£
Materials / resources	£	£
Advertising / marketing	£	£
Contingency fund	£	£
National Insurance	£	£
Pension	£	£
Total annual cost / Total weekly cost	£	£

INCOME

Now that you have worked out your expenditure, you can begin to work out how much income you are going to need to earn from your childminding business.

| YEARLY EXPENDITURE | ÷ | WEEKS AVAILABLE TO WORK | = | WEEKLY INCOME REQUIRED |

Now work out how much you will need to charge per place in order to cover your expenses. It is unrealistic to expect 100 per cent occupancy, especially when starting a business, so it is important to account for this when planning fees.

| WEEKLY EXPENDITURE | ÷ | REALISTIC NUMBER OF CHILDREN | ÷ | HOURS AVAILABLE | = | HOURLY FEE |

For example:

| £320 WEEKLY EXPENDITURE | ÷ | 2 NUMBER OF CHILDREN | ÷ | 40 HOURS AVAILABLE FOR THEM TO ATTEND | = | £4 HOURLY FEE |

In this example, the hourly fee of £4.00 has been calculated to cover weekly expenditure costs. If you choose to work out your hourly rate this way, check whether it is in line with other childcare providers in your area.

Some childminders find that they have higher costs in their first year of business, as they are having to pay for start-up costs, but in the second year they can start to earn more. Again, it is important to be realistic about the income you are going to need when deciding to start a childcare business and if you can survive the first year on less. You may wish to consider your start-up costs when working out your hourly fee, to recoup some of these costs over the year.

You will also need to allow for a contingency fund for times when your business may be quieter or not working at full capacity, such as the summer months when families tend to go on holiday. It is also a good idea to cover unforeseen future expenses, too, such as maintenance or repair work required for your setting. Use months when you have more income to set money aside for your contingency fund.

Monitoring your budget forecast is crucial as it enables you to react to changes by either reducing expenditure or increasing income as required, which may prevent future financial difficulties. It also helps you to ensure that you break-even at the end of each financial year, or in other words that your income matches your expenses. Any surplus can then be additional income or used to invest in the business.

❝ With a financial plan I can keep on top of my income and outgoings. I plan for future activities and it also ensures I meet my legal requirements such as paying tax and NI ❞

Emma Price, Hertfordshire

Fees and charges

We have looked at setting fees, but it is also important to consider how to manage the collection of fees and other charges that may apply. It is essential that you are clear with parents about what your fees are, when fees need to be paid and any additional charges that they may incur (for example, if you charge extra for the provision of nappies or food) from the very beginning.

A payment policy could be included in your admission/welcome pack and needs to be rigorous to cover when fees will be collected and arrangements in the event of late or non-payment. Having a policy agreed before any issues arise can improve communication and help to quickly resolve any misunderstandings.

PACEY recommends that childcare fees are collected in advance. The recommendation from PACEY's legal team is that a deposit is taken from parents at the beginning of any contract, or that they pay upto four weeks' fees in advance. Details of any deposit or advance payment should be agreed and included in the contract. Then, should the parents end the childcare arrangement without giving you notice or without paying you in lieu of notice, you may, under the terms of your contract, retain the deposit or advance payment against payment of the notice period.

If you are unable to offer a held childcare place as agreed, the deposit should be returned to the parent(s) in full.

If you are a PACEY member, find out more at
www.pacey.org.uk/childminding_contracts

In the case of late or non-payment, you may want to send a reminder letter, a warning of removal of the place or ultimately withdraw the place. We often find it difficult to talk about money, but this is your business and to be successful for all children it needs to be financially viable. Remember, you have a contract with the parents to offer a service and they have a contract with you to pay for that service.

TAX

As a new childminder, you will be self-employed and therefore need to understand the requirements and regulations around this. Childminders are generally, in business terms, recognised as a sole trader. More information on setting up as a sole trader can be found at www.gov.uk/set-up-sole-trader

You are required to register with HM Revenue & Customs (HMRC) and complete a self-assessment form for each year, detailing your income and expenses; and pay tax on any income over a certain amount set by HMRC each year (this varies depending on your circumstances). However, some of the money you spend running your business is called an "allowable expense" and can be claimed for tax relief. In other words, it can be deducted from your income and you will not need to pay tax on that amount of your income. There is no definitive list of what allowable expenses are, but the type of things you may claim for are:

- Food and drink consumed by the children
- Resources and equipment for the children (as long as these are purely used for the childminding role and not personal use)
- Fuel and car-related expenses when travelling with the children
- Advertising and marketing
- IT equipment required for the business
- A percentage of your utility bills
- Training and Continuous Professional Development (CPD) that is relevant to your role (not including initial training)

If you use a PACEY Accounts Book at your setting, you can find explanations about allowable expenses in the front. This way, you always have the information to hand when logging your accounts.

An agreement about childminders' expenses has been established by HMRC and PACEY. Visit www.hmrc.gov.uk

It is essential for you to keep clear records of income and expenditure, including receipts, and attendance records (a statutory requirement). Receipts are not required for items costing less than £10. Receipts are required if a number of smaller items are purchased at one time and the total cost is £10 or more. HMRC offers an e-learning course that covers topics such as tax, national insurance, business records and expenses. It can be completed at your own pace and at a time that's convenient for you. Visit www.pacey.org.uk/hmrc to find out more about the course and to view other useful links about tax and self-employment.

To find out more about paying National Insurance, visit www.hmrc.gov.uk/working

It is a good idea to open a separate business account to manage your business finances from. This will help you avoid mixing personal finance and business finance.

WORKING WITH OTHERS

A growing number of childminders are choosing to work in teams with other childminders and assistants. You can be self-employed and also employ others, but you must ensure that you understand the requirements concerning pay, insurance and working conditions. These include registering with HMRC as an employer. For further advice, visit **www.pacey.org.uk/factsheets**

Childminding assistants

A childminding assistant works with a childminder, caring for children on domestic premises, usually the childminder's home. A childminder may employ an assistant so that they can care for more children, or to give particular care to a child with specific needs. To find out more about working with a childminding assistant in England or Wales, visit **www.pacey.org.uk**

PACEY offers membership to childminding assistants, including free training, expert helplines, practice guides and videos to support childminding assistants to develop their skills, too.

FUNDING

England: Free Early Education

As a childminder, you may be able to access other sources of income such as early education funding and start-up grants.

Free early education is available for 3- and 4-year-olds, and disadvantaged 2-year-olds in England. All 3- and 4-year-olds are entitled to part-time funding until they reach statutory school age, for 15 hours a week for 38 weeks of the year. This is known as **Free Entitlement Funding (FEF)**.

A CHILD BORN ON OR BETWEEN	CAN ACCESS A FREE PLACE FROM
1 April and 31 August	1 September following the child's 3rd birthday
1 September and 31 December	1 January following the child's 3rd birthday
1 January and 31 March	1 April following the child's 3rd birthday

There is flexibility with how the entitlement can be accessed, but it must be taken over a minimum of two days a week or a maximum of five days a week. For further information, contact your local authority.

To access the funding, register on the directory of providers with your local authority. Families will need to complete a declaration form and you will be required to submit the information to the local authority by a specific deadline. This is called the Headcount Date. The Headcount Date is a specific date usually towards the beginning of each term. For each term claimed, a child must attend your setting on or before that term's Headcount Date advised by the local authority. Details of these dates should be available on your local authority website. You will not invoice the parents for the hours that they have FEF as the Government states that this should be free at the point of delivery.

Early education funding is also available for 2-year-olds from low income families. These places are offered to families on low incomes who are in receipt of at least one of the following:

- Income Support
- Income-based Jobseekers Allowance
- Income-related Employment and Support Allowance
- Child Tax Credit with income of less than £16,190 and not receiving Working Tax Credit
- Support under part VI of the Immigration and Asylum Act 1999
- Guarantee element of State Pension Credit

Children who are or have been in local authority care are also eligible. Some children with special educational needs and/or disabilities who require extra support can be referred by specialist services working with them. Again, you will need to register with your local authority and complete an application form.

More information can be obtained from your local authority or from www.gov.uk

From September 2014, 2-year-olds who meet any one of the following criteria are also eligible:

- If they meet the eligibility criteria also used for free school meals
- If their families receive Working Tax credits and have annual gross earnings of no more than £16,190 per year
- If they have a current statement of special educational needs (SEN) or an education, health and care plan
- If they attract Disability Living Allowance
- If they are looked after by their local authority
- If they have left care through special guardianship or through an adoption or residence order

Wales: Funding and grants

In Wales, free part-time early years education is available. How this is delivered varies from one local authority to another. Please check with your local authority for further details for your area.

Flying Start is the Welsh Government's Early Years programme for families in some of the most deprived areas of Wales. One element of the programme provides free part-time quality childcare for 2- and 3-year-olds. Again, how this is delivered varies from one local authority to another. Please check with the Flying Start team within your local authority for further information.

There may be grants and support available from your local authority and so it is always a good idea to check if there are funding streams available.

SUPPORT AND
FURTHER READING

PACEY RESOURCES

PACEY can offer members support with all aspects of establishing a successful childminding business, including:

- Business paperwork
- Insurance
- Training courses
- Expert helplines
- Factsheets
- Practice guides
- Practice videos
- Sample policies and procedures
- Magazine, e-newsletter and bulletin
- Peer support

Business paperwork

At PACEY, we understand the challenges of managing your own business. To make life a little easier, we produce a comprehensive range of resources and documents designed to help you run a professional business. All paperwork is available at discounted rates for PACEY members. These include:

- Childminding Contracts
- Childminding Assistant Contracts
- Accounts Book
- Attendance Register
- Childminders' Receipt Book
- Child Record Forms
- Journal

Insurance

Bluefin offers Homeminder and Motorminder insurance policies* which have been created in partnership with PACEY to cater specifically for childminders. Visit **www.bluefingroup.co.uk/pacey**

*Underwritten by Aviva

professional association for
childcare and early years

Training courses

Childminding is an ever-changing profession, in which you are always learning. PACEY has produced training materials tailored to your needs to help you grow professionally. The courses are designed to provide support if you are just starting out, and opportunities to build on existing skills.

PACEY has developed a range of free online training courses for members. The courses are designed to support your continuous professional development and are tailored to you and your home nation's framework, whether you work to the EYFS in England or the Foundation Phase in Wales.

To find out more about PACEY's free training courses,
visit **www.pacey.org.uk/training**

To find out about courses available to buy through PACEY,
visit **shop.pacey.org.uk**

Expert helplines

PACEY members benefit from expert help via three exclusive expert helplines:

- Childcare and early years
- Health and wellbeing
- Legal support

Find out more at **www.pacey.org.uk/benefits**

Factsheets

Factsheets have been developed by PACEY's team of expert associates. They are a simple way to grow your professionalism and keep your practice up to date. PACEY factsheets cover range of topics, from contracts to characteristics of effective learning. Visit **www.pacey.org.uk/factsheets**

Practice guides

PACEY practice guides clearly explain some of the most important elements of childcare. Written by PACEY's team of experts, the guides support members to meet the needs of the children in their care, using up-to-date techniques which can be easily communicated to parents.

Practice videos

PACEY has developed practice videos to show childcare professionals at work, demonstrating best practice in a range of subjects, from messy play to reflective practice. Visit **www.pacey.org.uk/videos**

Policies and procedures: England

As a registered childminder in England, you must have clear policies and procedures in place in accordance with the requirements of the EYFS. Although childminders in England are not required under the EYFS to make written copies of policies and procedures available, it is good practice for all home-based childcarers to have written policies, and to give copies of these to parents and carers.

PACEY has produced a series of sample policy and procedure documents which you can refer to for ideas when writing your own unique policies and procedures. These are only available to PACEY members and have been written to meet the requirements of the EYFS for childminders in England.

professional association for
childcare and early years

Policies and procedures: Wales

As a registered childminder in Wales, you must have clear policies and procedures in place in accordance with the Childminding and Daycare Regulations (2010) and requirements of the National Minimum Standards for Regulated Childcare (2012).

These policies and procedures must be in place before you register as a childminder, and your pre-registration course will cover how to write a policy. Download PACEY's guide to writing your policies and procedures (Wales). Visit **www.pacey.org.uk**

It is important that you take time to go through these policies with parents and carers during settling-in visits. This will help you and the parents to get to know each other and will give parents the opportunity to ask questions about your policies and procedures.

PACEY e-newsletters and practice bulletins

PACEY e-newsletters keep you up to date on the sector, policy news, PACEY developments and topical events, as well as new training and resources available through your PACEY membership. Monthly practice bulletins also deliver essential practice guidelines and topical resources to explore at your fingertips.

Membership magazine

The Childcare Professional magazine is produced exclusively for PACEY members and celebrates the working lives of childminders, nannies and nursery workers. Includes craft and creative ideas, research-based features and member interviews that reflect our readers' worlds.

Peer support

PACEY Local is our peer-to-peer support and online community network for early years and childcare professionals. As well as an online community, PACEY Local offers face-to-face meetings across England and Wales.

The local groups offer an opportunity to meet socially with other childcare professionals; to help each other with planning; or to attend drop-in sessions and local trips out with the children you care for.

The PACEY Local online community is another way to get involved, allowing you to connect with childcare professionals across England and Wales.

To find your local group, visit **local.pacey.org.uk/local-groups**

Find out more

If you are already a member of PACEY, visit **www.pacey.org.uk** and log into MyPACEY to find out more about the range of resources available to you. If you're not already a member, visit **www.pacey.org.uk/join**

EXAMPLES AND TEMPLATES

SWOT analysis example

STRENGTHS	WEAKNESSES
• Professional association membership • Early years training • Brought up my own two children • Have a large garden and good local resources • Big car • Really love kids • Have lots of friends with young children – good network	• Not very organised with accounts • New to marketing and selling a business • Nervous about dealing with difficult parents • No recent experience of caring for babies
OPPORTUNITIES	THREATS
• Support from PACEY • Support from local Early Years Consultant • Support from local children's centre • Local nursery is closing down • New housing estate being built – family centred so more families moving in	• New childcare businesses opening • Illness • Complaints to Ofsted/CSSIW • Parent leaving their job • Schools delivering more out of hours services

SWOT template

STRENGTHS	WEAKNESSES

OPPORTUNITIES	THREATS

PACEY members can download this template from **www.pacey.org.uk**

MARKETING PLAN EXAMPLE

Name of business: May's Childminding

Business description: (Describe the services you will be providing)
A childminding service for children from 4 months to 8 years, 5 days a week, between 7.30am and 6pm. Available 48 weeks a year. Overnight services and occasional weekend services available. French language practice also available. The setting is a family home with a garden and dedicated play and learning area. Situated in a large town with surrounding countryside, there is also plenty of scope for outdoor learning activities in the nearby parks and woodlands, as well as the extensive social learning resources such as soft play and activity areas. Fully qualified and Ofsted registered.

Pricing:
£4.50 per hour weekdays, negotiable for weekend and overnight services. Includes all food and toiletries.

Aims and objectives:
To provide a 'home from home' learning and development experience. I will work closely with parents to ensure each child receives the type of care their family prefers.
The first year marketing objective is to place two children within the first six months, expanding to four children by the end of the first year.

USPs:
- Level 3 Diploma
- Seven-seat people carrier
- Good outdoor space
- Out-of-hours service available
- French language spoken

Market research:
My local town has 150,000 residents, with approximately 50,800 homes. Almost 40 per cent of these households contain dependent children. There are 28 nurseries and pre-schools in the area, and around 150 registered childminders. Unemployment is low and of the people who are employed, around 75 per cent are employed on a full-time basis.

MARKETING PLAN TEMPLATE

Name of business:

Business description: (Describe the services you will be providing)

Pricing:

Aims and objectives:

USPs:

Market research:

PACEY members can download this template from **www.pacey.org.uk**

MARKETING ACTIVITY EXAMPLE

Launching my business:
Offer a 10% discount on first month's childcare. I have already surveyed parents of a local school and in surrounding area, and the results were very positive. Many said they would consider using my services and two parents have already asked for further information. Items already planned from 1 August are:

MARKETING ACTIVITY	MESSAGE	WHEN	COST
2 x door drops in my area to 2,000 homes	Childcare vacancies now available – give your children a 'home from home' when school starts again	Early August and again in late August	Delivery – free as my family is helping Print – £119 including online design from online printers for 4,000 leaflets
Poster in local children's centre	Childcare vacancies now available in caring, professional local setting	July, August, September	£10 a month – three-month trial £30
Card on supermarket 'local business' wall, and in various local shops – newsagents, café, hairdressers	As above	July, August, September	Check with each location

These prices are examples only

MARKETING ACTIVITY	MESSAGE	WHEN	COST
Advertising in local paper	Childcare vacancies now available in caring, professional local setting	July, August, September	£78 a month for box in childcare section of listings, total £234 for three-month trial
Free vacancy matching service through PACEY membership	Details of my service and availability	Ongoing	N/A
Online advertising in parents' area of website for local residents	Childcare vacancies now available in caring, professional local setting. Can pick up from local school	July, August, September	£100 design cost and £200 for 50,000 page impressions (about three months' worth)
Word of mouth	As above	Ongoing	N/A
FIS	Confirm details they are able to promote	Ongoing	N/A
Free online forums	Childcare vacancies now available in caring, professional local setting	Ongoing	N/A

MARKETING ACTIVITY	MESSAGE	WHEN	COST
May's Childminding website	A landing page which tells about my services and shows pictures of me and my setting Describes my qualifications and experience and the kind of childcare I will provide To include a 'contact me' enquiry form	Ongoing	£10 a month from a service where I use a template of my choosing and type my own text in £120 a year

Marketing budget for launch:
Initial costs for the three months of launch activity total approximately £713.

Ongoing costs will depend on vacancies available. Basic marketing including local restaurants and shops, advertising on the local parents site and maintaining my own website total around £86 a month.

MARKETING ACTIVITY TEMPLATE

Launching my business:

MARKETING ACTIVITY	MESSAGE	WHEN	COST

PACEY members can download this template from **www.pacey.org.uk**

MARKETING ACTIVITY	MESSAGE	WHEN	COST

PACEY members can download this template from **www.pacey.org.uk**

MARKETING ACTIVITY	MESSAGE	WHEN	COST

Marketing budget for launch:

PACEY members can download this template from **www.pacey.org.uk**

FINANCIAL PLAN EXAMPLE

My start-up costs will include the following:

Training	£325
Ofsted (If registering with CSSIW in Wales there is currently no charge)	£35
Disclosure and Barring Service (DBS) x 2	£108
PACEY membership and PLI insurance	£98
Marketing	£50
Website	£35
Resources and equipment	£300
Improvements to home (safety measures / accessibility)	£200
Total	**£1,151**

I have applied for a Government grant of £250

My annual expenditure will include the following:

PACEY membership and PLI insurance – circa	£100
Ofsted (If registering with CSSIW in Wales there is currently no charge)	£35
Repairs and replacement of equipment	£200
Percentage of utility bills	£200
National Insurance contributions	£109
Total	**£644**
Weekly breakdown	**£12.38**

My weekly expenditure will include the following:

Food and drink for the children	£45
Fuel	£30
Cleaning materials	£10
Resources	£7
Total weekly expenditure: (Approximate figure)	£12.38 (annual expenses broken down into weekly amount) £92.00 weekly expenditure / **Total = 104.38**
My charges will be:	£4.00 an hour

* For more examples of annual and weekly expenditure, turn to page 25.

FINANCIAL PLAN EXAMPLE

To cover my expenditure I will need to: (How many hours of childcare do I need to sell to cover my expenditure? How many children does this mean I will need to care for?)

I will need to sell at least 27 hours of childcare to cover my expenditure. This would equate to three children for nine hours a week each or four children for seven hours a week each (28 hours).

Additional notes

I would need to sell more hours a week to increase my contingency fund and to provide an income for myself.

I would also need to earn more in my first year if I am to cover my start-up costs.

SOURCES OF SUPPORT

Support	What can they support me with?
PACEY	Insurance, support, training, legal advice, factsheets, practice guides, best practice information via membership magazine and e-newlsetters **www.pacey.org.uk**
HMRC	Factsheets, online training **www.hmrc.gov.uk**
Local authority	Support and advice, advertising. Check opportunities for funding
Local childminding group	Approach for general support and advice

FINANCIAL PLAN TEMPLATE

My start-up costs will include the following:

	Total

My annual expenditure will include the following:

	Total
	Weekly breakdown

My weekly expenditure will include the following:

Total weekly expenditure: £
(Approximate figure)

My charges will be: £

PACEY members can download this template from **www.pacey.org.uk**